P9-DHG-465

SCIENCE DARES YOU!

MaKe FaKe BLOOD

And 18 more spooky special effects!

Cool fake blood!

Thank you.

by Sandra Markle
Illustrated by Eric Brace

SCHOLASTIC INC.

New York Toronto London Auckland Sydney
Mexico City New Delhi Hong Kong Buenos Aires

For two special young scientists, Molly and Pita Elliott—S.M.

For little Beth, the human fajita.—E.B.

The author would like to thank Leon Phillips, Professor of Chemistry, Canterbury University, New Zealand, for sharing his expertise and enthusiasm. As always, a special thank-you to Skip Jeffery for his help and support.

No part of this publication may be reproduced in whole or in part, or stored in a retrieval system, or transmitted in any form or by any means, electronic, mechanical, photocopying, recording, or otherwise, without written permission of the publisher. For information regarding permission, write to Scholastic Inc., Attention: Permissions Department, 557 Broadway, New York, NY 10012.

ISBN 0-439-44431-4

Text copyright © 2004 by Sandra Markle.
Illustrations copyright © 2004 by Scholastic Inc.
All rights reserved. Published by Scholastic Inc.
SCHOLASTIC and associated logos are trademarks and/or registered trademarks of Scholastic Inc.

12 11 10 9 8 7 6 5 4 3 2   6 7 8 9/0

Printed in the U.S.A.   40
First printing, January 2004
Design by Jennifer Rinaldi Windau

SCIENCE DARES YOU TO . . .

Get spooked! 5

Make glue bounce 9

Stab a balloon without popping it 12

Hang ice by a thread 17

Pour salt through a handkerchief 19

Float an egg in the middle of a jar 23

Make a cartoon appear on blank paper 25

Make dark pennies shine 28

Make an eggshell vanish 31

Shrink a naked egg 34

Mummify an apple 38

Make invisible ink appear 42

Trap a ghost in a bag 46

Make your mouth fizz 49

Make fake blood 53

Amazing spooky facts! 57

Dare yourself! 62

Note to Parents and Teachers: The books in the *Science Dares You!* series encourage children to wonder why and to investigate to find out. While they have fun exploring, young readers discover basic science concepts related to each book's theme. They also develop problem-solving strategies they can use when tackling any challenge.

In *Science Dares You! Make Fake Blood*, children tackle challenges that help them become empowered to ask questions and seek solutions. In the process, they develop an understanding about the nature of matter and how things in the world work. "A substance has characteristic properties. Substances react chemically in characteristic ways with other substances to form new substances with different characteristic properties." (National Science Education Standards as identified by the National Academy of Sciences.)

SCIENCE DARES YOU TO
GET SPOOKED!

Would you like to make an eggshell vanish, make a bag **inflate** as if by magic, or whip up a tasty treat that starts fizzing the instant it touches your tongue? Believe it or not, you can do all these things—*and lots more*—when you tackle the dares in this book.

All you need is some creativity, a little help from Science, and an amazing **part of the universe**: MATTER

The Basics

First, you need to know something about matter. Everything you see and touch in the world is made up of matter. It comes in three main forms, or states: solid, liquid, and gas.

All matter is made up of tiny building blocks called atoms that can be arranged in different ways. In a solid, the atoms are packed tightly together. This gives the solid a definite shape. In a liquid, the atoms are free to move around. The liquid can flow to take the shape of any container. In a gas, the atoms are spread far apart, but they can be pressed together to fill a space, like when air is blown into a balloon.

Heat or cold can make one form of matter change to another. That's what happens when water freezes and becomes ice or when it boils and turns into steam.

Sometimes, when two kinds of matter mix together, a reaction happens. That means that the two substances change in some way. One may dissolve, or break into bits that mix with the other. This is called a physical reaction. Or two or more kinds of matter may combine to form an entirely new and different kind of matter. This is called a chemical reaction.

be careful

STAY SAFE!

Always check with an adult partner to be sure the way you plan to meet each dare will be safe for you to try. Never, ever put anything you are testing into your mouth unless you know it's safe to do so.

You're almost ready to take the dares and find out why matter matters. But beware! You never know what can happen when you start messing with matter — things could get spooky! Before you get started, here are some tips that will help you meet each science challenge.

HELPFUL HINTS

Brainstorm ways to tackle the challenge. Use the clues provided to help you think of possibilities. Then list three to five things you could try.

Choose which ideas would be most likely to work. Don't forget to check with an adult to be sure your idea is safe for you to test.

Test your idea. Then read over the suggested way to meet the challenge. Try it, too. Then decide if this approach provides some ideas you might use to modify and improve your solution.

Now you're ready to get spooked. . .
if you dare!

MAKE GLUE BOUNCE

You can do it!
Just check out the clues.

Clues

✘ Study a rubber ball. Does the ball bounce? How will the glue need to change to be more like the rubber ball?

✘ Borax, a laundry freshener, is a chemical that will make the glue's atoms link together into long chains. How might this help you meet the dare?

Take the Dare!

You'll need:

Measuring cup
2 plastic cups
Water
Tablespoon
Borax (laundry freshener available at grocery stores)
White glue
Spoon
Adult Partner

WARNING!

✘ Borax is a poisonous substance.
✘ Be very careful when you handle it and <u>always</u> ask an adult for help.

1. Work at the kitchen sink. Pour one-fourth cup of water into a plastic cup.

2. Add one tablespoon of Borax and stir until most of the crystals are dissolved.

3. Pour one-fourth cup of white glue into the other plastic cup.

4. Add the Borax liquid to the glue. Don't add any of the crystals remaining in the bottom of the cup. Stir well to mix.

5. When you have a solid lump, push on it with the spoon to squeeze out any unmixed glue. Poke and squeeze until no more liquid glue is released.

6. Take the solid ball in your hands, and rinse it well under the faucet. Squeeze the rubbery mass over the sink to be sure any remaining liquid glue is released.

7. Shape into a ball, and drop the ball on the floor. Congratulations! It bounces, proving you've met the dare.

DOUBLE WOW!

In the 1940s, James Wright was trying to create a cheap substitute for rubber by combining silicone oil with boric acid. The result was a polymer that didn't replace rubber, but it turned out to be a great toy. Originally called "Nutty Putty" it's now called "Silly Putty." This compound is soft and easy to shape, but it also bounces almost 25 percent higher than a rubber ball. It can also stretch many times its length without tearing, picks up pencil marks from paper, and either floats or sinks depending on its shape.

What Happened?

Groups of atoms of the same kind of substance are called molecules. White glue is made up of long chains of molecules hooked together. When the white glue was mixed with Borax, a chemical reaction happened. This made the chains of glue molecules all link together like strands of yarn being knitted into a loosely woven cloth. And that made the glue behave like rubber.

WOW! Long chains of molecules are called polymers—and not all of them are manmade. Some, like rubber, occur naturally. Rubber is actually the sap of the Hevea tree. And while it's bouncy and stretchy, it isn't very useful. It gets sticky in hot weather and breaks apart easily in cold weather. But in 1839, inventor Charles Goodyear discovered an important chemical reaction. Mixing rubber with sulfur and heating the mixture made it change. The rubber-sulfur material stayed rubbery in all kinds of weather.

STAB A BALLOON WITHOUT POPPING IT

Sound impossible? You can do it —
once you know a secret about balloons.

Clues

✘ A balloon's skin isn't solid. The chains of atoms forming its skin have tiny spaces between them. How might you use this fact to meet the dare?

✘ Blow up a balloon and take a close look at it. Can you find any places where the stretched rubber looks thicker? Could these thicker spots help you meet the challenge?

Take the Dare!

You'll need:

3 rubber balloons
Vegetable oil
Sharp straight (sewing) pin

1. Blow up one balloon. Tie a knot in the neck to seal it.

2. Rub oil on the pin to make it slick.

3. Find the darkest spots on the face of your balloon. One should be close to the neck, and the other should be directly opposite that point. These are the two points where the balloon's skin isn't stretched quite as much.

4. Position the pin on the balloon over one of these dark spots. Hold the balloon so the pin is aimed away from you. (Be sure it also is not aimed at anyone else—just in case the balloon pops.)

5. Stab the balloon at one of the dark spots. If the balloon doesn't pop, you've met the dare!

6. If the balloon pops, coat the pin with more oil, blow up another balloon, and try again.

What Happened?

The balloon is made out of polymers, long chains of molecules. Where the balloon's skin is less stretched (the darker spots), the pin can slip between the chains of molecules. Don't believe a rubber balloon's skin isn't solid? Try this: Blow up a balloon, and tie it to seal it. Measure the distance around the balloon at the biggest point. Then measure the balloon again the next day and the day after that. The balloon will shrink, because air escapes between the molecules of the balloon's skin.

☜ A HISTORIC DARE ☞

IN THE LATE 1970s, the New York City Ballet Company wanted to use balloons for a special production number. So they needed balloons that would stay inflated for a long time. This led to the creation of a new type of balloon, called the nylon foil balloon, or mylar balloon. These shiny balloons stay inflated much longer than regular balloons, and are now very popular at birthday parties!

WOW!

An inflated balloon that's 3 feet (90 centimeters) across can lift about 2 pounds (1 kilogram)! How many balloons do you think it would take to lift you? (Warning: Don't actually try this at home!)

DOUBLE DARE #1

Science dares you to stick a bamboo shish kebab stick, or any other thin, pointy, smooth stick, all the way through a balloon.

Step 1.

Step 2.)

Step 3.

Step 4.

Step 5.)

HANG ICE BY A THREAD

It may seem like magic, but
you can meet this dare with
a little help from science.

Clues

✘ Have you ever touched something in the freezer and felt
your finger stick? That happened because your body heat
was enough to melt the surface of the spot you touched.
Then the melted ice quickly refroze. How might you use
making ice melt and refreeze to meet the dare?

✘ When winters are very cold, road crews sprinkle salt on roads
to melt the ice. How might salt help you meet the dare?

Take the Dare!

You'll need:

Ice cube
Metal cake pan
10-inch-long thread
Glass of water
Salt

1. Place an ice cube on the cake pan.

2. Dip one end of the thread into the glass of water, and pull
it out again.

3. Quickly coil the wet thread on top of the ice cube.

4. While you hold on to the dry end of the thread, sprinkle salt over the wet end.

5. Count to 20. Then slowly pull straight up on the thread. Just like magic, the thread sticks to the ice!

What Happened?

The salt melted the surface of the ice cube. This melting took heat energy from the air just above the cube and from the water on the wet thread. Enough heat was removed from the water on the thread to freeze it. That glaze of ice acted like glue, sticking the thread to the ice.

WOW!

You would have had a hard time meeting this dare in ancient times. Back then, salt was hard to come by. In fact, Roman soldiers were given salt as part of their pay. Even today, a hardworking person is said to be "worth his salt."

POUR SALT THROUGH A HANDKERCHIEF

Surprise yourself with this dare.
The clues will start you brainstorming
how to do it.

Clues

✘ When salt is stirred into water, it seems to disappear. What do you think happens to it?

✘ Wet clothes dry because the water evaporates, or moves into the air. How might evaporation help you meet this dare?

Take the Dare!

You'll need:

Tablespoon
Salt
Bowl
Hot tap water
Spoon
Quart jar
Clean handkerchief
Rubber band

1. Pour two tablespoons of salt into the bowl.

2. Add a cup of hot tap water.

3. Stir until the salt crystals are no longer visible.

4. Stretch the handkerchief over the top of the quart jar. Anchor it with the rubber band.

5. Pour the salt water into the jar through the handkerchief.

6. Set the jar in a warm spot, and remove the handkerchief.

7. Let the jar sit for several days, until the water disappears. When you see crusty salt in the bottom of the jar, you know you've met the dare!

What Happened?

When the salt mixed with the water, it dissolved. That means the salt molecules became suspended in the water. If you looked at the handkerchief with a magnifying glass, you would see it isn't solid. There are tiny spaces between the threads. The water carried the suspended salt molecules through the tiny spaces in the cloth. Then the water evaporated, leaving the salt behind.

WOW! Sodium and chlorine are both poisonous chemicals. But when these chemicals combine, they form a new kind of matter that's safe enough to eat—table salt. (Warning: Don't try this at home!)

FLOAT AN EGG
IN THE MIDDLE OF A JAR

You won't need a haunted egg.
A little science magic will do the trick.

Clues

✗ If you've ever been swimming in the ocean, you know it's easier to float in salt water than in freshwater. How might this help you meet the dare?

✗ Dissolving salt or sugar in water makes the liquid become denser (thicker). How might this help you meet the dare?

Take the Dare!

You'll need:

Quart jar
Warm tap water
Uncooked egg
Serving spoon
Tablespoons
Salt

1. Fill the jar two-thirds full of warm water.

2. Put the egg on the spoon, and lower it into the water.

3. Ease out the spoon, and watch the egg sink.

4. Take the egg out, and add two tablespoons of salt to the water. Stir until the salt dissolves.

5. Let the jar sit until the water stops moving.

6. Lower the egg into the water again. Presto! The egg will float this time.

7. Repeat, adding more salt, one tablespoon at a time, until the egg floats in the middle of the jar. When that happens, you've met the dare.

What Happened?

By dissolving salt in water, you made the water denser. Finally, the salty water was dense enough to support the egg in the middle of the jar.

WOW! You wouldn't have trouble floating an egg in the Dead Sea. The Dead Sea is actually a landlocked lake between Israel and Jordan. It has the saltiest—and densest—water on Earth. The water is 10 times saltier than any ocean. It's too salty for fish to survive there.

DOUBLE DARE #2

Science dares you to stack red water on top of blue water.

MAKE A CARTOON APPEAR
ON BLANK PAPER

Once you figure out how to do this you'll be able
to copy cartoons and comics to share with friends.

Clues

✗ Rub your finger across newsprint. Then rub your finger
across a clean paper towel and you'll see that you've
transferred some of the ink. Could rubbing help you meet
the dare?

✗ Put a scrap of a colored picture from the newspaper into a
cup and cover with a tablespoon of white vinegar. Check
after an hour and you'll see some of the printing ink has
dissolved, coloring the vinegar. How could this help you
meet the dare?

Take the Dare!

You'll need:

Cotton swab
White vinegar
Colored picture out of a comic book or the newspaper
(*Check with an adult to be sure you have permission
to cut out the picture.*)
Paper towels
Sheets of white typing paper
Metal spoon

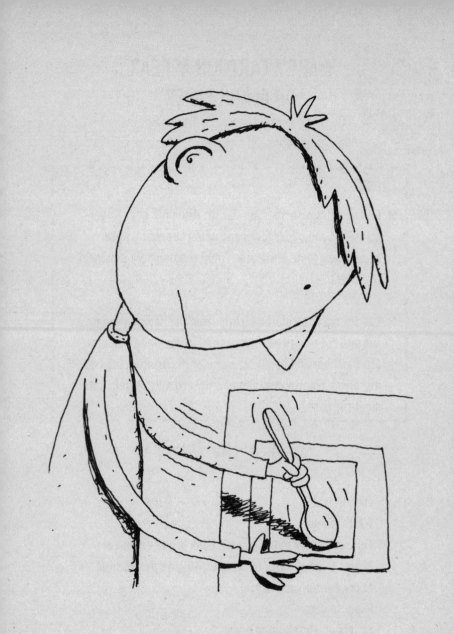

1. Use the cotton swab to spread vinegar all over the picture.

2. Press the picture between two paper towels to soak up any excess vinegar.

3. Place the picture, vinegar-coated side down, on a sheet of white paper.

4. Rub the picture briskly with the back of a spoon. Lift the picture to see the print. Although the colors will be paler, you'll have a copy of the original.

What Happened?

Some chemicals dissolve or break apart and become suspended in liquids. Many chemicals will dissolve in water, but not the permanent dyes used in printer's ink. However, vinegar is able to dissolve the ink. Rubbing forced the dissolved ink onto the white paper. Did you notice the print you made is a reverse image of the original?

WOW!

The earliest vinegar was spoiled wine or beer. In fact, the word vinegar comes from the French word **vinaigre**, meaning sour wine. History shows vinegar has been used since ancient times to prepare and preserve food. Vinegar has also been used as a medicine and a detergent. Now, you've found another use for it.

MAKE DARK PENNIES SHINE

Once you know how, you won't even have to touch the pennies to make them shine.

Clues

✗ Remember what vinegar did to dyes?

✗ Look at the pennies closely. Scratch the dark surface with a nail to see that only the penny's surface is dark.

Take the Dare!

You'll need:

Dinner plate or a sturdy paper plate
Five dark brown pennies
1 cup vinegar
2 tablespoons of salt

1. Place the pennies on the plate. Put them close together but not overlapping.

2. Sprinkle the salt evenly over the pennies.

3. Pour the vinegar over the salt-coated pennies. The pennies will change from dark to shiny copper, showing you've met the dare.

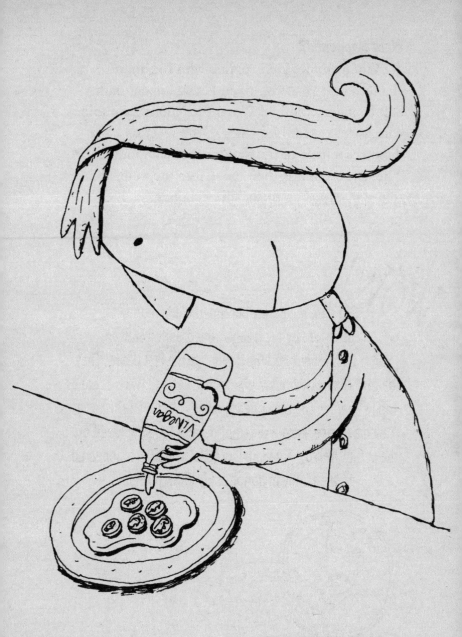

What Happened?

When copper is in contact with the air, it changes to copper compounds that appear dark. Salt contains chloride. When the chloride combines with a weak acid, like vinegar, the reaction dissolves a little of the dark copper compounds. These compounds then move into the vinegar solution, exposing fresh, shiny copper.

WOW!

In 1787, the penny became the first money authorized by the newly formed United States. Ben Franklin suggested the design for the first penny. That one-cent coin was about five times heavier and twice as big as today's penny. The name penny comes from the British coin called a **pence**. Eleven different designs have appeared on the penny. In 1909, Abraham Lincoln's portrait first appeared on the penny in honor of his 100th birthday.

Will you please clean me?

MAKE AN EGGSHELL VANISH

Don't worry! You can do this with
a little help from science.

Clues

✗ Place a small piece of eggshell in a tablespoon of vinegar,
and leave it overnight. The next day the piece of shell will
be soft and crumbly. Could vinegar help you meet this
dare?

✗ Do some research on "acids" in science books or on the
internet. What can you learn about acids that might help
you meet the dare?

Take the Dare!

You'll need:

Scissors
One-liter plastic soft-drink bottle
Uncooked egg
16-fluid-ounce bottle of vinegar

1. Cut the top off the soft-drink bottle.

2. Place the egg in the bottle.

3. Pour in enough vinegar to cover the egg.

4. Leave the egg covered with vinegar until the shell material crumbles when you rub the egg.

5. Rub the egg all over to remove the shell.

6. Rinse in a bowl of water. Congratulations! You've met the dare. Now, hang on to your "naked" egg. You'll need it to tackle the next dare.

What Happened?

Vinegar is a type of liquid called an acid. Acids can break down certain kinds of matter, like calcium carbonate, the main material in an eggshell.

WOW!

If you want to see a really big naked egg, start with an ostrich egg. It's the world's biggest bird egg—about eight inches (20 centimeters) tall and weighing more than three pounds (1,360 grams)!

DOUBLE DARE #3

Science dares you to bend a chicken bone.

SHRINK A NAKED EGG

No, you can't break the egg's
sturdy membrane (outside covering). You'll
have to figure out another way to meet this dare.

Clues

✘ The egg's membrane may feel solid, but it's really like a
screen full of tiny holes. How can this fact help you meet
the dare?

✘ Drip red food coloring in water, and watch the coloring
spread out until all of the water is tinted. Think about how
this reaction could help you meet the dare.

Take the Dare!

You'll need:

Tape measure
"Naked" egg
Sandwich-size self-sealing plastic bag
Corn syrup (or dissolve one-fourth cup sugar
in a cup of hot water)

1. Have an adult partner help you carefully measure the
distance around the naked egg.

2. Place the egg in the bag.

3. Pour in enough corn syrup to cover at least half of the egg.

4. Seal the bag.

5. The next day, take the egg out of the bag, and rinse it off. Then measure the distance around the egg again. Congratulations! The egg should be smaller, which means you've met the dare.

What Happened?

Think of a drop of red food coloring in a glass full of water. Matter always just naturally tends to spread out from where there is a lot of it, to where there is less of it. The egg's tough membrane is like a screen with tiny holes. So the water inside the egg flows out of the egg and into the surrounding sugar syrup. You might think the opposite would also happen — that the sugar molecules would flow into the egg. But they don't, because sugar molecules are much larger than water molecules. They are too big to fit through the holes in the egg's membrane. Since the egg lost molecules without gaining any new ones, it shrank.

A Historic Dare

IN ANTARCTICA, the only supply of water that isn't frozen solid is the ocean. Because that water is salty, no one can drink it. So scientists developed a process to remove salt from seawater. They pumped the salty water through a special membrane. This had openings so small it only let the water molecules pass through, and it blocked the salt molecules. Now scientists stationed in Antarctica have plenty of freshwater to drink.

DOUBLE DARE #4

Science dares you to make the naked egg swell up again.

MUMMIFY AN APPLE

In ancient Egypt, dead bodies were preserved by drying out the body's soft tissues. This process turned the body into a mummy. Your challenge is to do the same thing to an apple.

Clues

✗ Before refrigerators, meat was salted to keep it from spoiling. How might salt help you meet the dare?

✗ If you soak a slice of cucumber in saltwater for 15 minutes, it will become rubbery. Water inside the cucumber moves through its cell membranes and into the salty water. How might this process help you meet the dare?

Take the Dare!

You'll need:

Full container of salt
Mixing bowl
Peeled apple (You can use a pencil
to carve a face in the apple's soft tissue.)

1. Pour enough salt in the bowl to cover the bottom.

2. Set the apple on the salt.

3. Pour salt into the bowl until the apple is completely covered.

4. Leave the apple there for a week.

step 1

step 2

step 3

step 4

One month later

5. Dig out the apple. You'll see it's shriveled, proving it lost some moisture.

6. To get the apple really dry, you'll need to rebury it and leave it for as long as a month. Keep checking every week. When the apple looks and feels like leather, you've met the dare.

What Happened?

The water molecules inside the apple's tissues moved into the salt. That made the apple dry out. Of course, just exposing the apple to the air would have dried it eventually, but salt has another benefit. It contains a natural antibacterial agent— that means it kills some of the bacteria that cause soft tissues to rot.

A Historic Dare

Since ancient times, people have been using salt to preserve food. The ancient Romans used salt to preserve, or cure, meats, olives, vegetables, and cheese. If you've ever eaten bacon, sauerkraut, or pickles, you've eaten foods preserved this way.

WOW!

According to ancient records, drying a human body could take as many as 70 days. Instead of plain salt, the ancient Egyptians used natron, a crusty material left behind when inland seas dried up. Natron was like a mixture of table salt, baking soda, and powdered bleach. Natron worked even better than plain salt because it could break down body fats.

To preserve a human body, the internal organs were removed and the body was packed with natron. The outside of the body was also covered with natron. After the tissue turned leathery, the natron was removed, and the body was sponged off with water. Finally, the body was stuffed with wads of linen cloth soaked in pine resins. The ancient Egyptians then wrapped the body in linen strips. This created the body bundle that we call a mummy.

MAKE INVISIBLE INK APPEAR

To tackle this dare, you need an invisible message. So dip a cotton swab into milk, squeeze out the excess, and write a note to a friend on white paper. Once the milk dries, the message will be invisible. Now, figure out how to make it appear again.

Clues

✕ When milk becomes hot enough, it turns brown. How might you use this reaction to heat to meet the dare?

✕ Look around the house. Make a list of the heat sources that could be safely used to heat paper without setting it on fire. How might you use one of these heat sources to meet the dare?

Take the Dare!

You'll need:

Adult partner
Sunglasses for you and your adult partner
Lamp
Oven mitt

1. You and your adult partner should put on sunglasses.

2. Have your adult partner remove the shade from the lamp and switch on the lamp.

3. Have your adult partner put on the oven mitt and hold the paper just above the bulb.

4. Make sure the paper doesn't actually touch the bulb. As the paper heats up, the message will appear. And — presto— you've met the dare.

What Happened?

When the paper was heated, the chemical compounds in the milk that are normally colorless turned brown. You and your adult partner could also try ironing the paper to heat it.

A Historic Dare

DURING THE REVOLUTIONARY WAR, the American army needed a way to send secret messages. They met this dare by using invisible ink. First, a fake letter was written, using regular ink. Next, the invisible ink message was written between the lines of visible print. They didn't use milk; instead, they used a mixture of water and a chemical called ferrous sulfate. Just like milk, heating made this chemical turn brown. To read the secret message, the letter was held over a candle flame.

TRAP A GHOST IN A BAG

You'll know you've met this dare when a self-sealing plastic bag swells up. But watch out! The ghost might pop out of the bag!

Clues

✗ Open a soft-drink can. The fizz you hear is escaping carbon dioxide gas. List all the things you can think of that fizz. Could fizz help you meet the dare?

✗ Pour a tablespoon of vinegar onto a tablespoon of baking soda. This causes a chemical reaction that gives off carbon dioxide gas. How might you use this chemical reaction to meet the dare?

Take the Dare!

You'll need:

Paper towel
Scissors
Tablespoon
Baking soda
Sandwich-size self-sealing plastic bag
Vinegar

1. Cut a paper towel into fourths.

2. Place a tablespoon of baking soda on one piece of the paper towel.

3. Roll this into a packet, and twist the ends of the paper towel to keep the baking soda inside.

4. Place the paper packet inside the plastic bag.

5. Pour in two tablespoons of vinegar, and seal immediately.

6. When the bag swells up, you've met the dare.

What Happened?

When the vinegar soaked through to the baking soda, it caused a chemical reaction, and that released carbon dioxide gas. Since the bag was already full of air, adding carbon dioxide gas made it inflate. So while the result looked magical, it wasn't really a ghost that caused the bag to swell up.

WOW!

Burning fossil fuels, like coal, wood, and gasoline, releases carbon dioxide gas into the air. Scientists believe gas gets trapped in the atmosphere and may be trapping heat energy there, too. That could make the air surrounding the earth heat up. The effect is called global warming, and it could make the world warm enough for glaciers and the polar ice caps to melt!

MAKE YOUR MOUTH FIZZ

Be prepared to get spooked! When you meet this dare, the liquid in your mouth will start bubbling. Use the clues to start brainstorming.

Clues

✗ Check out the ingredients in powdered products that are used to keep cut fruit from darkening. You'll find they contain citric acid. How might this powder help you meet this dare?

✗ Your mouth contains a watery liquid, saliva. How might the saliva help you meet the dare?

Note: Check with an adult to be sure what you want to try will be safe for you to test.

Take the Dare!

You'll need:

Teaspoon
Baking soda
Powdered citric acid (used to keep cut fruit from turning dark)
Powdered sugar
Unsweetened powdered drink mix

1. Combine one teaspoon of baking soda with two teaspoons of powdered citric acid.

2. Add three teaspoons of powdered sugar and two teaspoons of any unsweetened powdered drink mix.

3. Mix well.

4. Working at the bathroom sink, scoop about a half teaspoonful of the powder onto your tongue.

5. When you feel the fizz, you've met the dare. To see your saliva bubbling, open your mouth and look in the mirror.

What Happened?

Your saliva dissolved the citric acid and baking soda. Then a chemical reaction happened. It released the carbon dioxide gas bubbles that formed the fizz. The powdered sugar and flavoring were just a tasty bonus.

WOW!

Imagine making soda just by dropping a tablet into a glass of water! That's what the Emerson Drug Company did in 1957. They combined fruit flavoring, sweetener, citric acid, and sodium bicarbonate into a tablet called Fizzies. Fizzies became an overnight success. The soda tablet fad continued until 1968, when the artificial sweetener used in Fizzies was suddenly banned. Scientists thought it could cause health problems, so Fizzies was pulled from the market. It was 1995 before a replacement sweetener, NutraSweet, made it possible to reintroduce Fizzies.

DOUBLE DARE #5

Science dares you to make milk fizz.

MAKE FAKE BLOOD

You can meet this dare by turning a glass of water into a bubbling brew of boiling blood.

Clues

✗ Think how a balloon is like a bubble. What will need to happen to produce soap bubbles?

✗ Think about the fizz you created on your tongue. How might creating fizz help you meet this dare?

Take the Dare!

You'll need:

Tall drinking glass
Warm water
Red food coloring
Tablespoon
Baking soda
Measuring cup
Vinegar
Plastic cup
Liquid soap

1. Set the glass in the sink so being messy won't matter.

2. Fill the glass nearly full of warm water.

3. Pour in enough food coloring to turn the water bright red.

4. Add one tablespoon of baking soda, and stir to dissolve.

5. Pour a half cup of vinegar into the plastic cup.

6. Add a tablespoon of liquid soap, and stir just enough to mix.

7. Dump the soapy vinegar into the baking soda water, and watch the action. Presto! You've met the dare.

What Happened?

The chemical reaction between the vinegar and baking soda generated carbon dioxide gas. And the escaping gas produced bubbles — lots of red bubbles.

WOW!

Imagine using soap to shape your hairstyle. Researchers have found evidence that the ancient Israelites mixed ashes with oil to produce a kind of soapy hair gel. It was probably the ancient Romans, though, who first used soap to wash clothes. The ancient Greeks made a soaplike material too, but they used it to treat skin diseases.

Amazing Spooky Facts!

IS THERE A CREEPY, ROTTING GHOST IN THE HOUSE? *If you smell a strange and foul odor it could be a natural gas leak. If there is a gas leak, any spark could cause an explosion. So since natural gas is naturally odorless, gas companies add a chemical to the gas, called methyl mercaptan, to give it an odor. This chemical comes from rotting animal flesh. It creates such a disagreeable smell that people notice as little as one billionth of a gram added to four hundred liters of gas. That way there's no doubt when there's a natural gas leak.*

IMAGINE SEEING A SLIMY YELLOW BLOB PULSATING as it slowly moves across the ground. That's nature's own slimy substance called slime mold. It's really a kind of fungus that feeds on bacteria and plant matter. As it feeds, its cellular material circulates around and around. This makes the slime mold pulsate and move. Eventually, the blob turns gray, becomes hard, and breaks down into brown powder. The brown powder is millions of tiny spores. Like seeds, these are carried by the wind to develop into new slime molds.

LEECHES WOULDN'T BE FOOLED BY fake blood. These aquatic worms live by sucking in the real thing. From the time of the ancient Greeks until the late 1800s, leeches were used as a medical treatment. It was believed that bloodletting helped cure diseases. So leeches collected from freshwater ponds and streams were placed on a patient's skin over a vein. There it was allowed to suck up about half an ounce of blood. Today, leeches are being put to work again. This time, leeches are being used to remove blood that builds up in tissue after a skin transplant.

#1 Poke the stick into one of the darker (less stretched) parts of the balloon. Then push it out through another dark spot. Be sure to oil the entire stick. If the balloon pops, try reinforcing the darker spots with transparent tape. Then try again.

#2 You discovered that water with dissolved salt is denser than freshwater. To meet this double dare, fill a glass half full of salty water and add blue food coloring. Next, add red food coloring to a glass of freshwater. Use a spoon to transfer red freshwater onto the surface of salty blue water. Since it's less dense, the red water will float on top of the blue water. Over time, though, you'll see the freshwater and saltwater mix where the two meet. When the mixing occurs, the colors will change.

#3 Like eggshells, bones are strengthened with calcium carbonate. For the fastest results, use a thin bone, such as a chicken wing bone. To remove the calcium carbonate from the bone, cover the chicken bone with vinegar. Test the bone after two days. If it still doesn't bend, put the bone in fresh vinegar. Repeat until the bone is bendable.

#4 You already discovered that water molecules easily move through an egg's membrane. So to make the shriveled egg swell again, place it in a glass of water. Let it sit overnight. You'll discover a swollen egg—probably larger than it was originally.

#5 Milk contains lactic acid, a weak acid similar to the acid in vinegar. So adding baking soda to milk will cause the same sort of chemical reaction. And carbon dioxide gas will be released, creating fizz.

DARE YOURSELF!

Congratulations! You've successfully met the dares presented in this book. You're not finished, though. Now, science dares you to use what you've discovered about matter, including: matter is made up of atoms, heat can change matter, and combining with other kinds of matter can cause a chemical reaction — it can even produce gas or an entirely different kind of matter. Then brainstorm and plan experiments to discover more about matter and chemical reactions. Just be sure to check with an adult partner that what you want to try is safe to test. Then let science help you meet all the dares you can dream up!

SCIENCE WORDS

ACIDS An important group of chemicals that are found everywhere in the world. Acids give foods a sharp taste. Fruit juices, milk, and tea contain weak acids. Acids can cause a chemical reaction when mixed with other types of chemicals.

ATOMS The tiny building blocks that make up all matter.

CARBON DIOXIDE A gas in the air. Animals produce this gas as a waste during activity. A flame cannot use carbon dioxide to burn.

CHEMICAL REACTION The process that happens when two or more kinds of matter interact.

DISSOLVE To cause matter to break down into bits that become suspended in a liquid, such as salt dissolving in water.

EVAPORATE To cause a liquid to change into a gas, such as when water changes into steam.

GAS A kind of matter that does not have a definite size or shape. A gas can expand indefinitely. It can also be compressed, as when air inflates a balloon.

LIQUID A kind of matter that has a definite size but doesn't have a definite shape. A liquid can change shape easily.

MEMBRANE A thin tissue that will let some but not all sizes of molecules pass through.

MATTER What everything in the world that you see and feel is made of. There are three types: solid, liquid, and gas.

MOLECULES The chemical building blocks of matter.

OXYGEN A gas in the air. It is used by animals and combined with food to release energy. It is necessary for fires to burn.

SALIVA A liquid produced in the mouth that helps the digestion process.

SOLID A kind of matter that has a definite shape and a definite size. A solid doesn't change shape easily.